Annual Planner

January	February	March
April	May	June
July	August	September
October	November	December

Goals

Key Objective _____

Goal Checklist

_____ ☐
_____ ☐
_____ ☐
_____ ☐
_____ ☐
_____ ☐
_____ ☐
_____ ☐
_____ ☐
_____ ☐

Places to Visit

_____ ☐
_____ ☐
_____ ☐
_____ ☐
_____ ☐

People to Meet

_____ ☐
_____ ☐
_____ ☐
_____ ☐
_____ ☐

Notes

Habit Tracker

Month
Year

Day

1
2
3
4
5
6
7
8
9
10
11
12
13
14
15
16
17
18
19
20
21
22
23
24
25
26
27
28
29
30
31

Monday	

Tuesday	

Wednesday	

Thursday	

Friday	

Saturday	

Sunday	

Every Day	

Monday	

Tuesday	

Wednesday	

Thursday	

Friday	

Saturday	

Sunday	

Every Day	

Monday	

Tuesday	

Wednesday	

Thursday	

Friday	

Saturday	

Sunday	

Every Day	

Monday	

Tuesday	

Wednesday	

Thursday	

Friday	

Saturday	

Sunday	

Every Day	

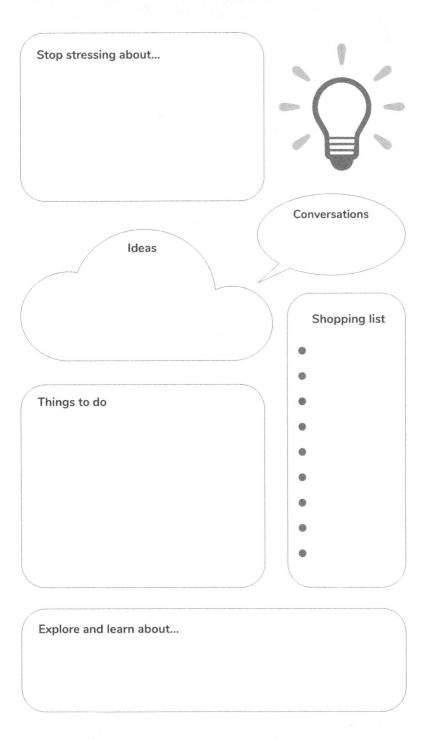

1.
2.
3.
4.
5.
6.
7.
8.
9.
10.
11.
12.
13.
14.
15.
16.
17.
18.
19.
20.

Key Objective _____

Goal Checklist

- [ ] _____
- [ ] _____
- [ ] _____
- [ ] _____
- [ ] _____
- [ ] _____
- [ ] _____
- [ ] _____
- [ ] _____
- [ ] _____

Places to Visit

- [ ] _____
- [ ] _____
- [ ] _____
- [ ] _____
- [ ] _____

People to Meet

- [ ] _____
- [ ] _____
- [ ] _____
- [ ] _____
- [ ] _____

Notes

Habit Tracker

Month

Year

Day												
1												
2												
3												
4												
5												
6												
7												
8												
9												
10												
11												
12												
13												
14												
15												
16												
17												
18												
19												
20												
21												
22												
23												
24												
25												
26												
27												
28												
29												
30												
31												

Monday	

Tuesday	

Wednesday	

Thursday	

Friday	

Saturday	

Sunday	

Every Day	

Monday	

Tuesday	

Wednesday	

Thursday	

Friday	

Saturday	

Sunday	

Every Day	

Monday	

Tuesday	

Wednesday	

Thursday	

Friday	

Saturday	

Sunday	

Every Day	

Monday

Tuesday

Wednesday

Thursday

Friday

Saturday

Sunday

Every Day

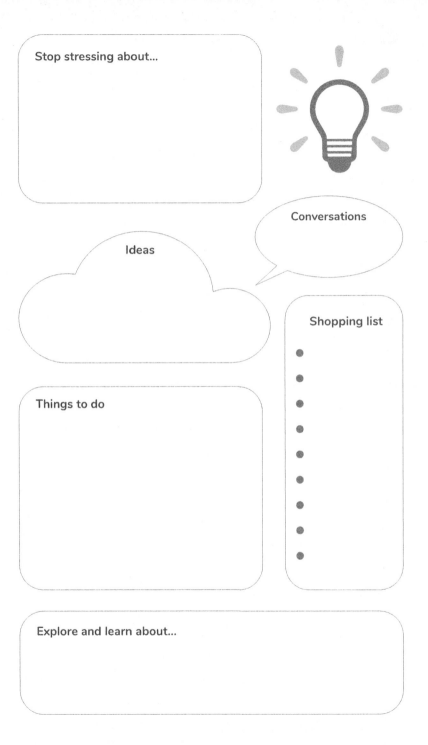

1.
2.
3.
4.
5.
6.
7.
8.
9.
10.
11.
12.
13.
14.
15.
16.
17.
18.
19.
20.

Key Objective _____

Goal Checklist

_____ ☐
_____ ☐
_____ ☐
_____ ☐
_____ ☐
_____ ☐
_____ ☐
_____ ☐
_____ ☐
_____ ☐

Places to Visit

_____ ☐
_____ ☐
_____ ☐
_____ ☐
_____ ☐

People to Meet

_____ ☐
_____ ☐
_____ ☐
_____ ☐
_____ ☐

Notes

Habit Tracker

Month

Year

Day												
1												
2												
3												
4												
5												
6												
7												
8												
9												
10												
11												
12												
13												
14												
15												
16												
17												
18												
19												
20												
21												
22												
23												
24												
25												
26												
27												
28												
29												
30												
31												

Monday

Tuesday

Wednesday

Thursday

Friday

Saturday

Sunday

Every Day

Monday

Tuesday

Wednesday

Thursday

Friday

Saturday

Sunday

Every Day

Monday	

Tuesday	

Wednesday	

Thursday	

Friday	

Saturday	

Sunday	

Every Day	

Monday

Tuesday

Wednesday

Thursday

Friday

Saturday

Sunday

Every Day

Stop stressing about...

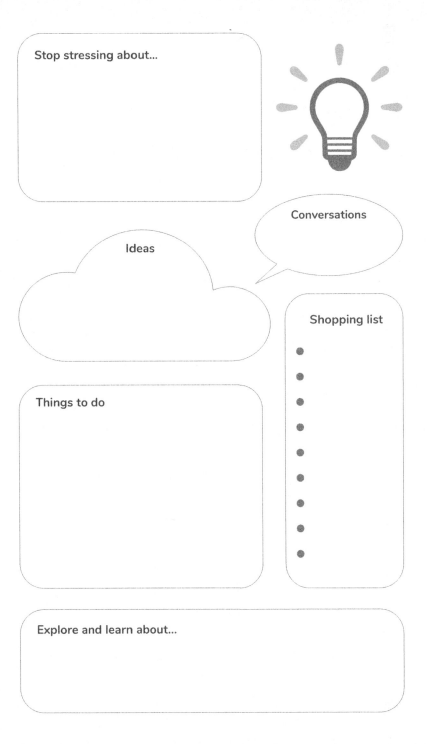

Ideas

Conversations

Shopping list

-
-
-
-
-
-
-
-
-

Things to do

Explore and learn about...

1.
2.
3.
4.
5.
6.
7.
8.
9.
10.
11.
12.
13.
14.
15.
16.
17.
18.
19.
20.

Key Objective _____

Goal Checklist

	☐
	☐
	☐
	☐
	☐
	☐
	☐
	☐
	☐
	☐

Places to Visit

People to Meet

Notes

Habit Tracker

Month
Year

Day

1															
2															
3															
4															
5															
6															
7															
8															
9															
10															
11															
12															
13															
14															
15															
16															
17															
18															
19															
20															
21															
22															
23															
24															
25															
26															
27															
28															
29															
30															
31															

Monday	

Tuesday	

Wednesday	

Thursday	

Friday	

Saturday	

Sunday	

Every Day	

Monday	

Tuesday	

Wednesday	

Thursday	

Friday	

Saturday	

Sunday	

Every Day	

Monday

Tuesday

Wednesday

Thursday

Friday

Saturday

Sunday

Every Day

Monday

Tuesday

Wednesday

Thursday

Friday

Saturday

Sunday

Every Day

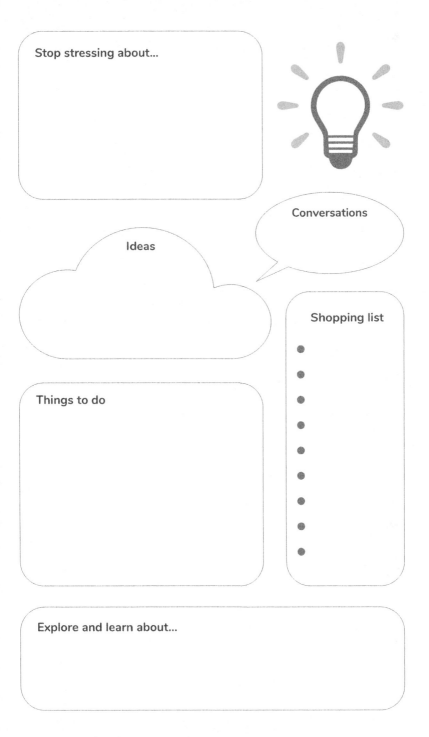

1.
2.
3.
4.
5.
6.
7.
8.
9.
10.
11.
12.
13.
14.
15.
16.
17.
18.
19.
20.

Key Objective _____

Goal Checklist

_____ ☐
_____ ☐
_____ ☐
_____ ☐
_____ ☐
_____ ☐
_____ ☐
_____ ☐
_____ ☐
_____ ☐

Places to Visit   People to Meet

_____ ☐   _____ ☐
_____ ☐   _____ ☐
_____ ☐   _____ ☐
_____ ☐   _____ ☐
_____ ☐   _____ ☐

Notes

Habit Tracker

Month

Year

Day

	1	2	3	4	5	6	7	8	9	10	11	12	13	14	15
1															
2															
3															
4															
5															
6															
7															
8															
9															
10															
11															
12															
13															
14															
15															
16															
17															
18															
19															
20															
21															
22															
23															
24															
25															
26															
27															
28															
29															
30															
31															

Monday	

Tuesday	

Wednesday	

Thursday	

Friday	

Saturday	

Sunday	

Every Day	

Monday	

Tuesday	

Wednesday	

Thursday	

Friday	

Saturday	

Sunday	

Every Day	

Monday	

Tuesday	

Wednesday	

Thursday	

Friday	

Saturday	

Sunday	

Every Day	

Monday	

Tuesday	

Wednesday	

Thursday	

Friday	

Saturday	

Sunday	

Every Day	

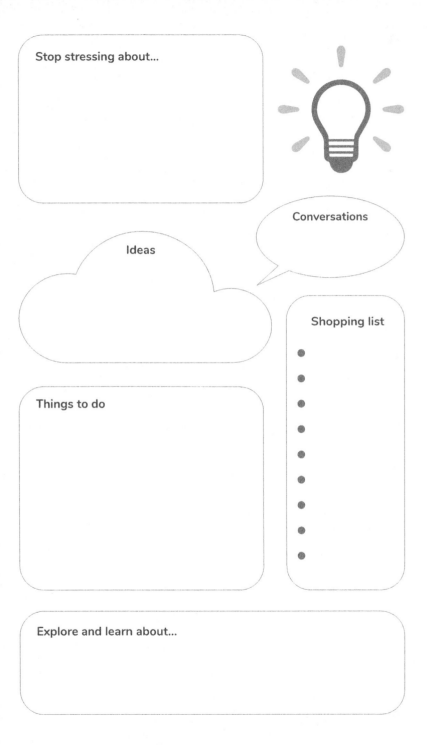

Key Objective _____

Goal Checklist

_____ ☐
_____ ☐
_____ ☐
_____ ☐
_____ ☐
_____ ☐
_____ ☐
_____ ☐
_____ ☐
_____ ☐

Places to Visit   People to Meet

_____ ☐   _____ ☐
_____ ☐   _____ ☐
_____ ☐   _____ ☐
_____ ☐   _____ ☐
_____ ☐   _____ ☐

Notes

Habit Tracker

Month _____

Year _____

Day

1																
2																
3																
4																
5																
6																
7																
8																
9																
10																
11																
12																
13																
14																
15																
16																
17																
18																
19																
20																
21																
22																
23																
24																
25																
26																
27																
28																
29																
30																
31																

Monday	

Tuesday	

Wednesday	

Thursday	

Friday	

Saturday	

Sunday	

Every Day	

Monday	

Tuesday	

Wednesday	

Thursday	

Friday	

Saturday	

Sunday	

Every Day	

Monday	

Tuesday	

Wednesday	

Thursday	

Friday	

Saturday	

Sunday	

Every Day	

Monday

Tuesday

Wednesday

Thursday

Friday

Saturday

Sunday

Every Day

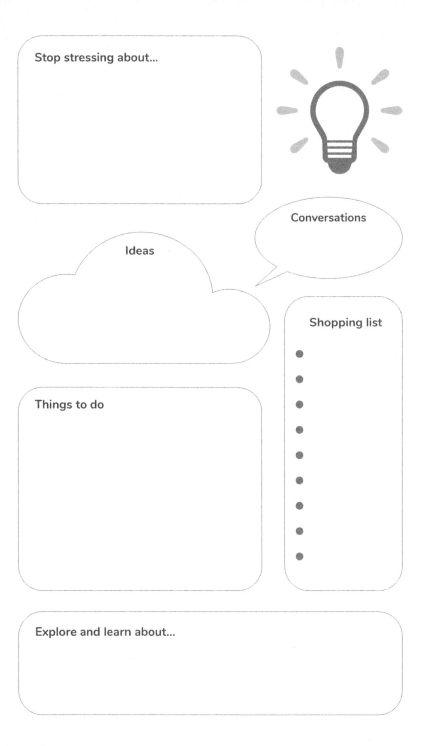

Key Objective _____

Goal Checklist

_____ ☐
_____ ☐
_____ ☐
_____ ☐
_____ ☐
_____ ☐
_____ ☐
_____ ☐
_____ ☐
_____ ☐

Places to Visit

_____ ☐
_____ ☐
_____ ☐
_____ ☐
_____ ☐

People to Meet

_____ ☐
_____ ☐
_____ ☐
_____ ☐
_____ ☐

Notes

Habit Tracker

Month

Year

Day														
1														
2														
3														
4														
5														
6														
7														
8														
9														
10														
11														
12														
13														
14														
15														
16														
17														
18														
19														
20														
21														
22														
23														
24														
25														
26														
27														
28														
29														
30														
31														

Monday	

Tuesday	

Wednesday	

Thursday	

Friday	

Saturday	

Sunday	

Every Day	

Monday	

Tuesday	

Wednesday	

Thursday	

Friday	

Saturday	

Sunday	

Every Day	

Monday	

Tuesday	

Wednesday	

Thursday	

Friday	

Saturday	

Sunday	

Every Day	

Monday	

Tuesday	

Wednesday	

Thursday	

Friday	

Saturday	

Sunday	

Every Day	

Stop stressing about...

Ideas

Conversations

Shopping list

Things to do

Explore and learn about...

Key Objective _____ ★

Goal Checklist

_____ ☐
_____ ☐
_____ ☐
_____ ☐
_____ ☐
_____ ☐
_____ ☐
_____ ☐
_____ ☐
_____ ☐

Places to Visit

_____ ☐
_____ ☐
_____ ☐
_____ ☐
_____ ☐

People to Meet

_____ ☐
_____ ☐
_____ ☐
_____ ☐
_____ ☐

Notes

Habit Tracker

Month
Year

Day
1
2
3
4
5
6
7
8
9
10
11
12
13
14
15
16
17
18
19
20
21
22
23
24
25
26
27
28
29
30
31

Monday	

Tuesday	

Wednesday	

Thursday	

Friday	

Saturday	

Sunday	

Every Day	

Monday	

Tuesday	

Wednesday	

Thursday	

Friday	

Saturday	

Sunday	

Every Day	

Monday	

Tuesday	

Wednesday	

Thursday	

Friday	

Saturday	

Sunday	

Every Day	

Monday	

Tuesday	

Wednesday	

Thursday	

Friday	

Saturday	

Sunday	

Every Day	

Stop stressing about...

Ideas

Conversations

Shopping list
-
-
-
-
-
-
-
-
-

Things to do

Explore and learn about...

Key Objective _____

Goal Checklist

_____ ☐
_____ ☐
_____ ☐
_____ ☐
_____ ☐
_____ ☐
_____ ☐
_____ ☐
_____ ☐
_____ ☐

Places to Visit

_____ ☐
_____ ☐
_____ ☐
_____ ☐
_____ ☐

People to Meet

_____ ☐
_____ ☐
_____ ☐
_____ ☐
_____ ☐

Notes

Habit Tracker

Month

Year

Day															
1															
2															
3															
4															
5															
6															
7															
8															
9															
10															
11															
12															
13															
14															
15															
16															
17															
18															
19															
20															
21															
22															
23															
24															
25															
26															
27															
28															
29															
30															
31															

Monday	

Tuesday	

Wednesday	

Thursday	

Friday	

Saturday	

Sunday	

Every Day	

Monday	

Tuesday	

Wednesday	

Thursday	

Friday	

Saturday	

Sunday	

Every Day	

Monday	

Tuesday	

Wednesday	

Thursday	

Friday	

Saturday	

Sunday	

Every Day	

Monday	

Tuesday	

Wednesday	

Thursday	

Friday	

Saturday	

Sunday	

Every Day	

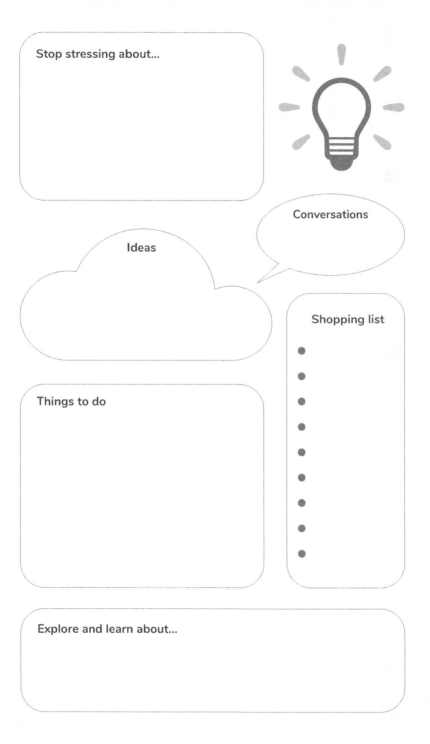

Key Objective _____

Goal Checklist

_____ ☐
_____ ☐
_____ ☐
_____ ☐
_____ ☐
_____ ☐
_____ ☐
_____ ☐
_____ ☐
_____ ☐

Places to Visit

_____ ☐
_____ ☐
_____ ☐
_____ ☐
_____ ☐

People to Meet

_____ ☐
_____ ☐
_____ ☐
_____ ☐
_____ ☐

Notes

Habit Tracker

Month
Year

Day

1
2
3
4
5
6
7
8
9
10
11
12
13
14
15
16
17
18
19
20
21
22
23
24
25
26
27
28
29
30
31

Monday	

Tuesday	

Wednesday	

Thursday	

Friday	

Saturday	

Sunday	

Every Day	

Monday	

Tuesday	

Wednesday	

Thursday	

Friday	

Saturday	

Sunday	

Every Day	

Monday	

Tuesday	

Wednesday	

Thursday	

Friday	

Saturday	

Sunday	

Every Day	

Monday	

Tuesday	

Wednesday	

Thursday	

Friday	

Saturday	

Sunday	

Every Day	

Stop stressing about...

Ideas

Conversations

Shopping list
-
-
-
-
-
-
-
-
-

Things to do

Explore and learn about...

Key Objective _____

Goal Checklist

_____ ☐
_____ ☐
_____ ☐
_____ ☐
_____ ☐
_____ ☐
_____ ☐
_____ ☐
_____ ☐
_____ ☐

Places to Visit

☐
_____ ☐
_____ ☐
_____ ☐
_____ ☐
_____

People to Meet

☐
_____ ☐
_____ ☐
_____ ☐
_____ ☐
_____

Notes

Habit Tracker

Month _____
Year _____

Day												
1												
2												
3												
4												
5												
6												
7												
8												
9												
10												
11												
12												
13												
14												
15												
16												
17												
18												
19												
20												
21												
22												
23												
24												
25												
26												
27												
28												
29												
30												
31												

Monday	

Tuesday	

Wednesday	

Thursday	

Friday	

Saturday	

Sunday	

Every Day	

Monday	

Tuesday	

Wednesday	

Thursday	

Friday	

Saturday	

Sunday	

Every Day	

Monday	

Tuesday	

Wednesday	

Thursday	

Friday	

Saturday	

Sunday	

Every Day	

Monday	

Tuesday	

Wednesday	

Thursday	

Friday	

Saturday	

Sunday	

Every Day	

Stop stressing about…

Ideas

Conversations

Shopping list
-
-
-
-
-
-
-
-
-

Things to do

Explore and learn about…

1.
2.
3.
4.
5.
6.
7.
8.
9.
10.
11.
12.
13.
14.
15.
16.
17.
18.
19.
20.

Key Objective _____

Goal Checklist

_____ ☐
_____ ☐
_____ ☐
_____ ☐
_____ ☐
_____ ☐
_____ ☐
_____ ☐
_____ ☐
_____ ☐

Places to Visit

_____ ☐
_____ ☐
_____ ☐
_____ ☐
_____ ☐

People to Meet

_____ ☐
_____ ☐
_____ ☐
_____ ☐
_____ ☐

Notes

Habit Tracker

Month
Year

Day													
1													
2													
3													
4													
5													
6													
7													
8													
9													
10													
11													
12													
13													
14													
15													
16													
17													
18													
19													
20													
21													
22													
23													
24													
25													
26													
27													
28													
29													
30													
31													

Monday	

Tuesday	

Wednesday	

Thursday	

Friday	

Saturday	

Sunday	

Every Day	

Monday	

Tuesday	

Wednesday	

Thursday	

Friday	

Saturday	

Sunday	

Every Day	

Monday	

Tuesday	

Wednesday	

Thursday	

Friday	

Saturday	

Sunday	

Every Day	

Monday	

Tuesday	

Wednesday	

Thursday	

Friday	

Saturday	

Sunday	

Every Day	

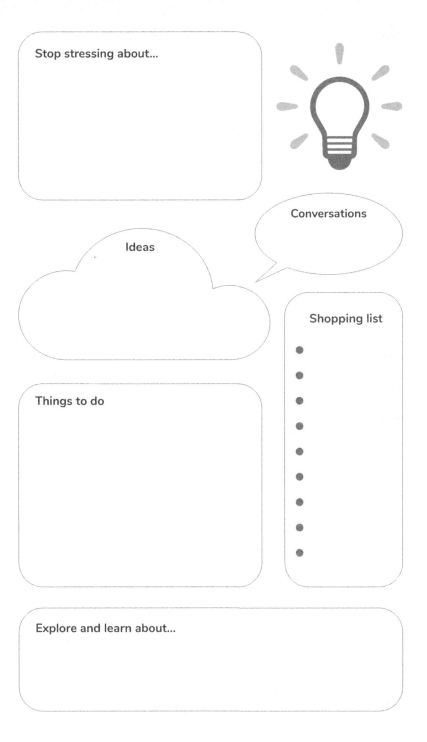

Key Objective _____

Goal Checklist

_____ ☐
_____ ☐
_____ ☐
_____ ☐
_____ ☐
_____ ☐
_____ ☐
_____ ☐
_____ ☐
_____ ☐

Places to Visit

_____ ☐
_____ ☐
_____ ☐
_____ ☐
_____ ☐

People to Meet

_____ ☐
_____ ☐
_____ ☐
_____ ☐
_____ ☐

Notes

Habit Tracker

Month
Year

Day											
1											
2											
3											
4											
5											
6											
7											
8											
9											
10											
11											
12											
13											
14											
15											
16											
17											
18											
19											
20											
21											
22											
23											
24											
25											
26											
27											
28											
29											
30											
31											

Monday	

Tuesday	

Wednesday	

Thursday	

Friday	

Saturday	

Sunday	

Every Day	

Monday	

Tuesday	

Wednesday	

Thursday	

Friday	

Saturday	

Sunday	

Every Day	

Monday	

Tuesday	

Wednesday	

Thursday	

Friday	

Saturday	

Sunday	

Every Day	

Monday	

Tuesday	

Wednesday	

Thursday	

Friday	

Saturday	

Sunday	

Every Day	

Stop stressing about...

Ideas

Conversations

Shopping list
-
-
-
-
-
-
-
-
-

Things to do

Explore and learn about...

Made in United States
North Haven, CT
07 August 2023